Receipts

Receipts from a Life

MICHAEL ELTERMAN

Tellwell Talent
www.tellwell.ca

ISBN
978-0-2288-7704-2 (Paperback)

TABLE OF CONTENTS

Afternoon

Evening

Dedication

I want to dedicate this book to my wife, Marion. After 50 years of knowing her, she is still the most loving, selfless, and supportive person I have ever met. I dedicate this book also to my 3 sons who have provided us with so much pride, joy, and purpose in life.

March, 2022

INTRODUCTION

A Receipt is a written acknowledgment that something of value has been transferred from one person to another. I once read that your words are the receipts you leave behind when your time is spent. These are your proofs of lived experience.

As you read my poetry, it may seem that I am a sad person. I am, in reality, a happy, grateful, fortunate person but I tend to write down what I experience when I'm in that other morose frame of mind. Perhaps we are most creative with an undercurrent of sadness. This poetry may not be great poetry but it is my honest and raw thoughts and feelings during a slice of time in my life.

There are few things in life that live up to their hype. I have found that being a parent to be singularly beyond my expectations. Freud said that our basic nature is about Sex and Aggression. Jung said that it is man's search for Spirituality. Adler concluded it is social. If I wrote a book on this topic I would say that our basic need is to give and receive Love. It is the only proverbial "true thing". Showing love is the act of mirroring and high-beaming back to others our regard for them. When life beats us down and our sense of self becomes dark, this is what we need to keep going. Perhaps people are different, but I can say with certainty that for myself my primary purpose and motivation has been my love for my family. Let my poetry be my Receipts that I'm giving you for giving me something of the greatest value.

Michael Elterman

Morning

ODE TO A CUPCAKE

When cupcakes grow to be muffins
They decide to just be themselves as
Nature intended them to be.
No longer needing the frosting.
Gone are the sprinkles.
Giving up their bright colours.
Still holding onto their paper cup
That hides their stretch marks.
Slower and more deliberate.
Bran and your health are now
What gives their life meaning.

THE HIPSTER

You sit there with your tight skin and judgement.
Self-satisfied and smug.
Pulling at a carefully pruned beard
Chai latte poured in your own mug.

You know all the newest restaurants
Artisan bread, cheese and beer
A vegan who loves charcuterie
Supermarket food makes you sneer.

You are into social media
You get all your news from on-line
You read about the world's tragedies
But this morning you feel-just fine.

Your resumes are sent far and wide
To look for just the right placement.
Your parents are nice enough
But want you out of their basement.

OUR SPACES

Do our spaces miss us when we are not there.
When we are gone do they feel more bare
Do our rooms feel gloomy
Do they feel too roomy
When we are gone too long do they even care?

TAKE CARE

Take care of my heart
Try not to let it break.
I never knew love until I saw you.
I never knew fear
Until I saw your little body.
I imagined you crossing roads-
Riding a bicycle-
Unkind people being mean.
Your hurt would be my pain.
I had to mute my fears
To let you live.
Take care of my heart.

DESIDERIUM

"A feeling of loss or grief for something
You once had and lost and can't find again"
That's what they call it.

All I know is that
I just miss you every minute
Like a table missing a chair
Like a splinter in my brain
That is always always there.

MY HOUSE

When we met you were new and fresh
Two little boys bounded the stairs
Big lawns back and front
Paba, Paba they yelled
Yes it's our new house.

Then teenage boys would trudge in:
I am home, there is food. I am safe.
Small bough burns around the doors
"Remember that's where" ...we said.
Memories of time together
Leaving home. Coming home.
Home is the container of family memory.
A big multi-chambered heart
We all live inside together.

REGRETS

Some painful regrets
We would rather forget.
You have to be a certain old
To catch them in your net.

I now wish I had told my father
how I felt.
All the things
left unsaid.
That still go round
now that he is dead.

Before I pass into memory
And you are whispering
"I thought I would see him again"
Say what needs saying
So you have no regrets
When you too are old men.

YOUR EYES

In your eyes I see the face of my bride
I see our new baby cry
I see you smiling with love
I see faraway sunsets together
In your eyes.

When I look in your eyes
I see the sadness of a hundred goodbyes.
I see the tears life caused you to cry
I see the passing of the years
In your eyes.

THE LETTER

It lies in the post-box so patiently
Like a sleeping snake.
An icicle to my chest.
A sudden rush of adrenaline.
Panic. I hear my pulse in my ear
Relax...perhaps it is nothing.
Breathe I tell myself.
I see that dreaded purple print but
Maybe the address is wrong?
No... That is me
The snake is awake.

A letter from the College.

THERAPY

You want me to help
Understand you.
Why you are a such a wreck.
You want me to plumb
The depths of your mind.
My dear, I fear that if I dived in
I might just break my neck.

TOO LATE?

Is it too late to try?
Am I still able to do it?
I am the oldest now
That I have ever been.
A year from now
I won't be more ready
I won't be more steady
Do it now
while I am still keen.
It's never too late to be
What you might have been.

WHO SAYS?

Who says I have to fit
What you think I am?
I am not always right
But I am never wrong.
I can be brutally peaceful
And peacefully savage.
I can be a motherly father
And a fatherly son.
I may not be what you expect
But I promise to be genuinely fake.

OAKRIDGE

Grey old couple
sitting at the Food Fair.
Silently but together
A dishevelled unmatched pair.
Grey sweatpants and runners
A nod, a glance, a smile
Held together by memories
Of a time when going out
felt more worthwhile.

TEARS

Tears of grief
Tears of compassion
Tears of joy.

Overflowing and spilling as
Evidence of an inner world
That breaches the banks of
The River of Life.

A drop in the ocean of emotions.
Secretions from an inner world
Flowing. Then gone with a wipe.

LITTLE CHILDREN

Whatever your child sees and hears
They try to find the meaning.
Whatever they understand
Is how they see the world.
This is who they are becoming.

Those little eyes and ears
Which struggle to understand
See all and hear all.
Take care and be aware
There's a person in-training in there.

HOME

Sometimes Home is a place.
Sometimes Home is a person.
Sometimes it is just a feeling.
When I am here with you
I know I am Home.

FORGIVENESS

I don't need you to be sorry.
I don't need your apology
For me to forgive you.

If I don't let go
My thoughts will blow the kindling
Of my anger until I burn a hole
In my own heart.

I will forgive you for me
It is something I must do.
If you can't get to forgiveness
I will carry a lot of shit for you.

ALONE

Feeling like the last lonely suitcase
Going around a carousel
Forgotten or discarded?
T'is too early to tell.

THE RIDE

As youth we wait anxiously in line to ride
Ticket in hand we shuffle forward
Some cut in line ahead. Some drop out.
We see the outline of the ride but
Not yet the feel.

Now I can see the faces of the riders
Some squealing with happiness
Others tight with dread and fear
Who will I be? Who will be my partner?
Will I be okay at the end?

My turn now to do what others did.
Watching the ride and then riding
Shows us who we are.
The anticipation of the climb
The exhilaration of feeling the Flow.
How we react to each twist and turn
The fear of falling and the relief of living.

As the ride slows and I see where it ends
I so want to ride again
But you only get one ticket.
Now I tell you who are still in line:
Ride with yours eyes wide open.
Remember as much as you can.
Find someone nice to ride with.

ENOUGHNESS

It descends on me like vapour
A hint at first and it grows
Until I say "there it is".
When it settles your body knows.

It could be my mood
It could be good food.
It could be with little ones
It could be my wife and sons.

It is feeling you have enough
It is a moment not to miss.
You just know life doesn't get better
You think "If this isn't nice, what is?"

LUCKY MAN

If you had a childhood that makes you smile and not angry.

If going to work every day means more than just getting a pay cheque-
You are a lucky man.

If you look back and feel it was mainly time well spent-

If when bad things happen you can put it behind you quickly and move on-
You are a lucky man.

If you are able to travel the world and come home and say 'there is nowhere I would rather be'-
You are a lucky man.

If you are long married and still feel they are the best person you ever met-
You are a lucky man.

If the person you aspire to be best matches how you feel when you are with them-

When your children seem to enjoy seeing you rather than doing it as a duty or a mitzvah-
You are a lucky man

MAKING TIME

How we spend our hours
Is how we spend our days.
How we spend our days
Is how we spend our years.
How we spend our years
Is how we spend our lives.

Every second of the day is
A decision and
A priority
This or that.
Now, next or later.

It is never whether we
"have" the time for it.
But always if we
"make" the time for it.
It is water that runs through our fingers.
We only make time if we cup it in our hands
And say, "here this is for you".

THOUGHTS FROM PUSHKAR

If all I can control is the now
I must break free and stick to a vow.
To leave my pond and swim in the ocean.
Free of the shoulds childhood set in motion.
Never to be one of the wilted Tilley men
Who have
Retreated to a mental bomb shelter just
Waiting for the end.

KILLING TIME

Time is killing me.
While I am killing time.
The shadow cast back from death
Makes me ask what I will regret
When I take my last breath.

When we are touched by death
We briefly refocus on life
And see what is fragile and brief.
We make promises to correct
What our mind has chosen to neglect.

While living long is a common goal
Living slow and living wide
Makes you look deep inside.
Consider how you want to live
Should life tomorrow give you the shiv.

RESOLVE

Let no man sway
What you need to say.

Say what you think
Don't be afraid to be loud.

To lead the orchestra you have to turn your back on the crowd.

GRATITUDE

You need to think
At least once a week
For what you have
And not for what you seek.

Being grateful for everything
No matter how small.
Smooths bumps in your road
Like nothing at all.

COMING HOME

Coming home to you
Is like a soft warm bed and
The first bite of ice cream.
It is a bee returning to a hive.
And a Roomba returning to its dock.

THE FARMER

You plant a seed to see it grow
With care you feed and worry
In sun and rain you stress and toil.
To all others you must say "sorry".

Now with strong thick roots
Nothing is more satisfying
Than to see your healthy fruit
Feed others and be thriving.

HAPPY BIRTHDAY OUR WONDERFUL SON.

ARRIVALS

Like anxious parents
With children leaving school.
They jockey and jostle for position
Some holding back as if too cool.
With strained necks and lifted heels.
The tension builds before the bell
The baggage is on the carousel.

FLIGHT ATTENDANT

Your girlish dreams of glamor
Are long since gone and dead.
Those fantasies of being
A Sky Goddess have all been
Put to bed.
You find yourself a flying waitress
With bunions and a frown
Waiting for retirement
Wearing "bus face" and feeling down.

THE THIRD LITTLE PIG

I fear bad things
Happening to you.
If I don't take charge
I fear it will all go askew.

I am the third little pig.
The triple stitch in your coat.
The Plan C guy.
A high castle with a moat.

I don't want to be alone
Of this I am quite certain.
But my fear of loss is great
That's me behind my curtain.

While I might seem controlling
And always patrolling,
Remember that it is love and fear
That constantly wants to draw you near.

SORRY

If I could only bite back my words
I would swallow it with my pride.
I just wanted to make them laugh
Not to tear you up inside.

A fat joke to a new bride.
I do not want you as my foe.
Only those of us who go too far
Find out how far you can go.

SNORING SPOUSE

I know you don't mean to let me down
When your snoring keeps me up.
Your sawing lets me curse and frown
When my precious sleep you disrupt.

I know you are my loving spouse
I couldn't love you more.
But at night when you keep me up
I could strangle you...for sure.

WORK

I have burned the candle
At both ends.
I may not last the night.
But both my friends and foes agree
My candle burned so bright.

TWO QUESTIONS

When all is said and done
Life only asks us two questions
Which we have to answer
Every minute of every day.

1. **Decide what matters to you.**
2. **Decide what kind of person you want to be.**

That's it.

THE WIND

It grew in my awareness
Like a brown cat creeping by.
It then pounced on my senses
And brought a tear to my eye.

Why are yours so very rancid
And mine so pleasantly benign.
Next time you decide to pass gas
Open a window...give me a sign.

REVIEW WRITTEN FOR JUST RIGHT RENOVATIONS

I am grateful to Just Right Renovations for teaching me a new language. It is called "Reno-speak". It sounds like English but it uses a different clock and calendar. For example: "The job will take 3 weeks" means "it will take 3 months", "if you have a repair we will get to you in 48 hours" means "we will do it in 3 months", "Friday" means "Monday", and "9am" means "11.00am". You get the idea. I am sure that this language is spoken widely here and around the world. If you have a project and want to also learn Reno-speak I can't think of a better company than Just Right to teach you.

DIVORCED FATHER

He thought it was for them all
To work two jobs for so long
She wasn't home when he would call
Working too much was his downfall.

Now he sees them every two weeks
Aside from the tearful drive-by peeks.
Her boyfriend now sleeps in his bed.
Their "new dad" is eating his bread.

We had it all he says to his friends
Now I can barely keep up my end.
He clearly sees the mistake he made
He can't believe the price he paid.

Afternoon

HOLD MY HAND

Your tiny hand
Holding mine as we walk.
Remembering
My past in the present.
As mine was held before.

That tiny hand that held so tight
Is now holding his own.
Those soft little fingers
Now do the work of a man.

Why am I here?
Why does every existential thought
Track back to you?

You are the one's I want to please.
The one's I want to applaud me.
Let's walk together one more time

Then let me go.

ALL THE TIME

When we were very young
You said that all you wanted
Was to be with me.

I have learned since then
That one sign of love
Is to want to be with that person.

Now that I am older and wiser
And understand much more
All I want to do is be with you
All the time.

WAKE UP

As a young father I would disappear
When fun or work flew me away.
My lovely little boys at home
Won't know I'm gone I would say.

In motels with green shag rugs
Trying to avoid being food for the bugs.
But I had time to think what was dear
Down time into my heart to peer.

It would bubble up from where
It's not clear,
I would startle myself
And exclaim-
"Why-the-fuck am I here?"

ARE YOU OK?

I could hear it in your voice
The tone gave me alarm
I felt the dread of adrenalin
I want to protect you from all harm.

No matter what was said or done
I am always on your side.
A parent is only as happy
As their least happy child

BUT I WISH IT WERE NOT SO

You never call to just say 'hi'
You never call when you are down.

I never hear a 'How are you?'
If I don't call you never do.

Sometimes at night I lay in my bed
Thinking of the things that arc lcft unsaid.

There's no point now in keeping score
I had just hoped that there might be more.

GOLDEN BOY

We gladly gave the best of us
In every possible way.
Your dreams were our dreams
Our Golden Avatar we would say.
Then you went away to grow and learn
And we hoped you would return.
We remained close from afar
But afar is still far away
So we could only yearn.

Not quite sure how we should feel
We try maintain an even keel
Our Masterpiece now
Hangs in someone else's gallery.
With Gods little joke must we deal.

LITTLE OWL

Little Owl with wise eyes
Who takes it all in
And just smiles
Understanding all while
Posing as a baby.

Turgid smooth arms
You just wait while
The brothers poke and coo
Until they realize they aren't
The boss of you.

WEEKEND IN APRIL (2016)

It is only when you have a child
You really learn about love and fears.
No one else could reduce me
To a puddle of pathetic tears.

I am a Jewish father you see
Who's sole purpose in his life
Is to try to get and give love to
His precious children and his wife.

TO GRANDCHILDREN
I NEVER MET

I left too early
And you came too late.
For us to know each other.

You might hear about me
And how I loved you all
Just ask Grammy and your father

I am dreaming of you now
My absence this will not sever,
I hope you have a great life.
I will love you all forever.

MY WIFE

We met as children
Or so it feels
Our youths we gave each other.
We see the world in a similar way
As we found the world together.

A better friend I have never had
With you nothing could I lack.
I was happy that you let me lead
As you always had my back.

MY CAT

We never know how you feel
As you keep this to your self.
You need to see everyone's cards
Where you hold yours we cannot delve
I wish we knew what's on your mind
Your thoughts and feelings as such
Do you not care at all or
Do you care too much?

EMPTY NEST

Your childhoods we gave our
Every thought.
More time with you
We now will have gladly bought.
Then you left with a little
backward glance and wave.
Leaving us like a ship without
the ocean.
Like a sailor without the sea.
Greying orphaned children.
Not still believing
That the best is yet to be.

RUBY CHEEKS

Ruby round cheeks you make us smile.
It's not your turgid fingers
Or your little fat thighs.
What we love most about you is
Looking again into your papa's eyes.

We know you from your pictures.
We can't get to you by car.
We hope you have the best life and
We will love you from afar.

In time we will grow to love you
For the person that you are.
In the meantime let us love you
As our child is your Paba.

HAPPY 35

I thought I knew what love is
'Til your little face did I see.
Then nothing was the same again
Nor could it forever be.

For the first time I knew real passion
My temper before was so calm.
I now knew I could kill or die
To keep you from all harm.

I have lived with only one purpose
To give you every chance.
I even tried give you extra
For your enjoyment to enhance.

You gave to me my Ikigai
A purpose to my life.
Nothing has been more useful
To cut through life's dross like a knife.

HAPPY 36

In the last year you became Paba
To a little boy we love
Stop and enjoy this moment
And be grateful to God above

Your time now is filled with work
It could rob you of your joy
The illusion of this will take years to see but
Savour every moment with little boy.

Thirty-six is double life
Dean you are so dear
Have a very happy birthday
And another wonderful year.

IT GOES FAST

We spend our time collecting money
Wasting time as if it will go on forever
But you don't know how fast it goes
Until you realize that it's over.

As a young father older people said
Enjoy them now...it won't last long.
And now I'm saying to you my son
It goes fast -and then it's over.

CYPRESS STREET

With the world outside infected
And danger lurks from others
Our little world stays unaffected
We peer out and pull up the covers.

We can't control what's out there
The doorbell makes us quiver
Will the next package kill us?
Will we wake up with a fever?

Let's keep our little world apart
Our island we hope will keep us
We know what's happening out there
But for now, let's live on Cypress.

YEARS OF LOVE

We thought we were old enough
To marry?
We thought we understood
"Forever"?
We fell in love with a feeling
And only met much later.

Through struggles and fears
Losing people who were dear.
We Diapered then Doctored 3 sons.
We gave them the best
Their success became our life quest.
You did, you gave, you made.
You fetched, you carried, you paid.
Never measuring what you got back
Your baggage was not others to pack.

As women get older
What was beauty in their soul
Starts to show on their faces
As age forgets to take its toll.

Your sweet, kind soul was flawless
Which is why I think you are now...
so gorgeous.

KIND BOY

Kind boy.
With your little raspy voice
And your gentle soul.
A core of steely resolve
That flashes up and fades.

Little light fingers
Who stands and watches.
You know more than you say.
I see you. Never change.

VERY GRAND DAUGHTER

Your name means night
But you are as bright as day.
Smooth and round.
Little pixie girl.
When you smile
It is like a ray of sun
Breaks through clouds
And warms the room.

BOSSY ELBOWS

Bossy elbows and busy legs
Plastic dotty boots
Little pumping legs
Talking furiously for us to hurry
"Gooly-Gooly" she says
Stopping just long enough
To make sure we are close behind.

THE HEART SEES NO WRINKLES

From 16 to 60 is much of our lives
Most of that time a mother and wife.
I have never known anyone
Who thinks of others so much.
Love in action with all that you touch.

Life that grinds others down
Has not challenged your ardor.
To make others lives better
Only makes you try harder.

Your children possess
the same loving souls.
Even if they lived north of the pole.
Even if they lived over the sea.
Marion's sons they will always be.

When I look at your face
Even after time, life and space
I see
The beautiful soul I saw from the start
That same keen, hopeful girl
Who made a home in our hearts.

FATHERHOOD

Welcome to Fatherhood!

There is no going back as this is a transformational threshold.

If you do it right you will feel that someone else's life is more important than your own.

You will experience great joy and pride but you will also experience fear and dread about this person's safety and well-being. I can't say enjoy the ride because you are both the passenger and the operator of this roller coaster.

The importance of everything else you do from now onwards pales in comparison. You will experience primal feelings you didn't know you had. Perhaps you will understand better now how I feel about you.

Pa

Written to my son on December 30, 2018.

ADULT CHILDREN

Although I still see you as 10
In my mind
I know you are men.

You no longer need me
To show you the way.
I just want to express
More than I say.

If it seems I am more quiet
And have put my words on a diet.
Be certain my love will endure
Of that you can be sure.

MY SON IS 41

Little children hanging from you
Like a tree with heavy ornaments.
Gloves, hoods and sleeves flying.
Long days and early mornings.

Droopy eyes and peanut butter smears
Also smiles, hugs and splashy baths.
Little bodies climbing on you
'Don't leave Paba' as you close the door.

What feels like it will never end
Ends.
The best of time but you don't know it
Yet.
Only the work remains.
It fills the hours but not the heart.

The heart is big but its openings are
Small.
That's why only little fingers can fill
The void.

TURNING 62

When you are young it feels
Like it will always be that way.
That someone else will pay.
That you could never turn grey.

No longer angular and taut.
I am slower and rounder
Chipped away by life lessons taught.

It helps to have a loving wife
And grateful children in your life.
Even if I am not getting younger
I know my heart will not die of hunger.

50 YEARS OF LOVE

From 16 to 66 is 50 years
It's been a lot more laughs than tears.
I am glad we found each other
Could not be happier with another.

Lovers don't meet in the world
They were together from the start.
There is a cosmic force from birth
That pulls like magnets of the heart.

I cannot remember not knowing you
If there was ever a time that I did.
I knew you were out there waiting
And I was waiting too but just hid.

Thank you for 50 Years of Love.
Last Saturday in February 1971-2021

ROUGH EDGES

All the rough edges are worn down
From years of knocking and grinding
Like stones in a tumbler.
Life together now is soft and smooth.

We no longer need to make a point
Who cares who was right?
Let's us be us again.
Let's kiss goodnight.

Like a hand in a glove
Like a tongue in a mouth
We glide and we flow
We learned with time "just let it go".
Life is better in peace
More laughs and less tears.
We see what's important
No more unrealized fears.

Even if rounder and smoother
The heart still skips a beat and
The pace quickens
Before we expect to meet.

Evening

NEXT TIME

See you next time...
Au revoir!
Auf Wiedersehen!
Arrivederci
Catch you later...

Had I only known...
I would have savoured our time
I would not have taken for granted
Next time will not extend to forever

We deny the fragility of our lives
How careless.
How presumptuous we are that
there will be a next time.

SIXTY-EIGHT

Taking my foot off the Accelerator
But not yet hitting the Brakes.
Not yet invisible like old people are
Closer to who I was-than who I am.
Not old enough for schoolgirls
To stand up for but
Old enough to be looked through by
the young.
Young enough to believe that 68 is
"The new Middle-Age"
Old enough to know it's not true.

GRANDCHILDREN

Life is strange that way
It starts with just you and a wife.
Then you live your life
And when it feels all over
These little familiar faces
Become the raisins
In the pudding of your life.

BOTTOM LINE

When all is said and done
The only source of grief is love.
Do I hold back or let it flow
When I find out I will let you know.

TOO SOON

I know I won't wake up one day
You know you will not too.
It's hard to imagine not being here
I know you also do.

I know it is bound to happen
No point to question why
Just enjoy the little time we have
To deny it would be a lie.

Don't think of me as dying too young
Whispered sadly in a hush.
Just think of me as leaving early
To try avoid the rush.

LET'S HOLD ON

Now that the children are gone
And no little bodies to hold
Let's hold onto each other
Until we are bleary and old.

CARRY ME

I knew one day you would carry me
Just as I carried you.
I did this with joy and
Without a frown
Now it is your turn
to be the last three to let me down.

ALWAYS WITH YOU

You have all meant so much to me
You know life is shorter than it seems
When one day I enter history
And am someone who has been
I know you won't forget me as
I will visit you in your dreams.

LIVING LIFE AS IF

What pervades my mind
Is the tiny voice and
Knowing wink
Constantly crouching
Underneath my awareness
That pulls me between
Living life
"As if I will live forever"
and Living Life
"As if I will die tomorrow".

Like a shuttle between two
Distant worlds
We have to live as if
Both Are true.
With one eye on each
switching eyes
Changes the perspective.

IN MEMORY

You are gone suddenly and forever
They cry and see where you sat and stood.
They see what you owned
And will never own again.
Sooner than expected you slip from view
Passing into history where you now live.
They stand looking into the grave
Like dogs barking into the void
Reminded that they will be there too.
Then, as they must,
Those left behind can't move on.
As like silent software always running.
They must move forward with you
In memory.

REAL THINGS CLIENTS
HAVE SAID TO ME

So I told my son, "I'm the one who puts food on your back!"

I told the kid, "Time to wake up and smell the coffee on the wall".

I asked "Do you still have sexual relations?" Client: "Yes, my sister-in-law has good legs!"

"My mother had 5 sons...all born by circumcision".

"I tried to come here in my girlfriends truck but she died on me".

"He is a child who wears his arm on his sleeve".

"I just want to be sure we have all our ducks on the same page"

How far did you go in school? Client: "About a kilometre from my house".

I asked: What did your father do for a living? Client: He was a surfer?
Me: That's interesting! Where did he surf? Client: Oh, he surfed at McDonalds.

What was your father like? Client: "Oh he like fishing... he like the tv..."

Me: Were you quiet or outgoing as a child? Client: "Yes outgoing...I outgoing on my bike...I outgoing to my friend".

Me: Were you teased as a child?

Client: Yes I was teased about being fat.

Me: Did that affect you?

Client: "No, I just rolled with it."

Client: My brother-in-law nearly choked this weekend at my house.

Me: What did you do?

Client: "I gave him the Heineken".

Client: "I couldn't make it last week because I had to drive my wife to the 'groin-a-cologist"

Me: Around what age were you bullied?

Client: Around the pubic area.

I am transitioning through a sex change right now. I will make an appointment once I tie up some loose ends.

I paid $10,000 to that sperm bank. When COVID hit they closed and gave me back my deposit.

I left you with a smile didn't I?

CPSIA information can be obtained
at www.ICGtesting.com
Printed in the USA
LVHW051128190722
723853LV00006B/291